Dent, Dasha, *You Are a Star!*

Copyright 2019 by Dasha Dent.

Cover and interior illustrations by Damien Dugger.

Published by KWE Publishing, P.O. Box 635, Prince George, VA 23875. www.kwepub.com. Contact at kwe@kwepub.com.

ISBN (hardback) 978-1-7326273-8-3

First Edition. All rights reserved. No part of this publication may be reproduced in any means, electronic or mechanical, including recording, photocopying, or any information storage or retrieval system, without written permission of the author. The exception would be in the case where permission is specifically granted by the author.

Although every precaution has been taken to verify the accuracy of the information contained herein, the author assumes no responsibility for any errors or omissions. The author shall have neither liability nor responsibility to any person or entity with respect to loss or damage caused, or alleged to have been caused, directly or indirectly, by the information contained in this book.

Dedication

This book is dedicated to every child. No matter who you are and no matter what you look like you have a light to shine. Always remember "You Are a Star" and you're one of a kind.

Preface

I wrote this book for all of the beautiful children in the world. This book is to show all children that they are talented and should never dim their light inside. Know that you can do anything that you put your mind to no matter how big or small it may seem, do it because you believe. Children teach me to always find the beauty in the small things and to never lose the child that is within me. Thank you to every child for continuing to be an inspiration to me.

Each one of them are special in their own way.

Stars of different colors, having one of a kind gifts.

Brown, white, purple, orange, green.
These are the stars you see.

Every star was hand picked
to shine in its own way.

Some have the gift of art.

Some have the gift of standing up and not being shy.

Some are good at spelling bees.

Some stars love to play hide and seek.

The list goes on and on of how these stars give off their light.

Sadly, some creatures like to dim the stars light.

But once the stars see that they are one of a kind.

Shining brighter than a shooting star.

Take a look at the beautiful star you are,

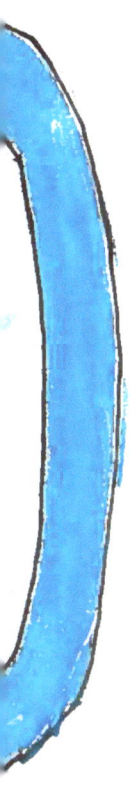

you're lighting up
the world by just being
who you are.

DASHA DENT is a children's book author, entrepreneur, and a crafter at heart. She is the founder of Books on Purpose which highlights that every book has a purpose and hopes to help other up and coming authors to take the leap of faith into writing that book. She's a child advocate that hopes to encourage children to use their voice and talents in their own unique way. "If you have a book inside, do not let it pass you by. You never know if that book could change someone's life." To learn more about Dasha Dent you can find her at www.bksonpurpose.com.

DAMIEN DUGGER, the illustrator of "You are a Star," is from Dinwiddie, Virginia. He has been drawing for a majority of his life. He has entered and won places in several art competitions, and has created murals for local businesses. He wanted to challenge himself because he's used to drawing complex detailed references. Mr. Dugger eagerly accepted the challenge of illustrating "You Are a Star," and he loved the experience. His goal is to illustrate more books with Ms. Dent, who is his cousin and the author of this book, as he appreciates the simple but strong message in this Ms. Dent's book.

CPSIA information can be obtained
at www.ICGtesting.com
Printed in the USA
LVHW070018221119
637662LV00014BB/503/P